New Jersey's Southern Shore

An Illustrated History from Brigantine to Cape May Point

Susan Miller

4880 Lower Valley Road, Atglen, PA 19310

Dedication

This book is dedicated to those members of my family, past and present, who have helped make New Jersey's Southern Shore such a wonderful part of my life.

Acknowledgements

I want to thank my husband, Fred, for his knowledge, support, and help; Stu Sirott for his technical know-how and hard work; and my sister and brother-in-law, Joan and Allan Okin, for their editing skills.

I also want to thank the Wildwood Crest Historical Society, Margaret Kickish, Kathleen Revelle, and Brigantine City Hall for providing me with information; the Ocean City Historical Museum, the Ocean City Lifesaving Museum, and Bruce Tell, of the Avalon Museum & Historical Society for providing information and allowing me to have use of their postcards.

Mary Lois Hughes and Sue Wright deserve much thanks for their gifts of postcards, which were used for this book.

I also thank J. Scott Ruch and Gwen and Bruce Riordan for lending me postcards from their collections.

Other Schiffer Books by Susan Miller
Ocean City, An Illustrated History, 978-0-7643-2709-4, $19.95

Other Schiffer Books on Related Subjects
The Ocean City Boardwalk, 0-7643-2455-1, $19.95
Cape May Puzzle, 978-0-7643-2725-4, $14.95
Greetings from Cape May, 978-0-7643-2678-3, $24.95

Designed by rOs
Type set in Souvenir LT BT

ISBN: 978-0-7643-3009-4
Printed in China

Schiffer Books are available at special discounts for bulk purchases for sales promotions or premiums. Special editions, including personalized covers, corporate imprints, and excerpts can be created in large quantities for special needs. For more information contact the publisher:

Published by Schiffer Publishing Ltd.
4880 Lower Valley Road
Atglen, PA 19310
Phone: (610) 593-1777; Fax: (610) 593-2002
E-mail: Info@schifferbooks.com
For the largest selection of fine reference books on this and related subjects, please visit our web site at **www.schifferbooks.com**
We are always looking for people to write books on new and related subjects. If you have an idea for a book please contact us at the above address.

This book may be purchased from the publisher.
Include $3.95 for shipping.
Please try your bookstore first.
You may write for a free catalog.
In Europe, Schiffer books are distributed by
Bushwood Books
6 Marksbury Ave.
Kew Gardens
Surrey TW9 4JF England
Phone: 44 (0) 20 8392-8585; Fax: 44 (0) 20 8392-9876
E-mail: info@bushwoodbooks.co.uk
Website: www.bushwoodbooks.co.uk
Free postage in the U.K., Europe; air mail at cost.

Contents

Introduction 5

Chapter One: Brigantine 7

Chapter Two: Atlantic City 13

Chapter Three: Ventnor 23

Chapter Four: Margate 29

Chapter Five: Longport 35

Chapter Six: Ocean City 43

Chapter Seven: Strathmere 57

Chapter Eight: Sea Isle City 63

Chapter Nine: Avalon 77

Chapter Ten: Stone Harbor 85

Chapter Eleven: The Wildwoods 93
North Wildwood, Wildwood, & Wildwood Crest

Chapter Twelve: Cape May 117

Chapter Thirteen: Cape May Point 123

Bibliography 127

Index 127

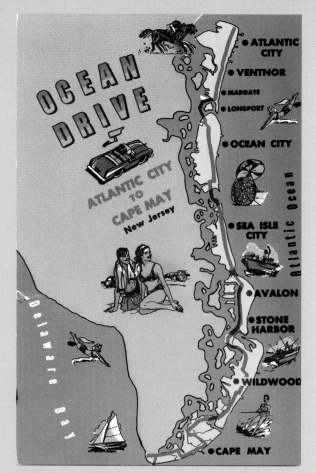

Map of Ocean Drive. Most of New Jersey's Southern Shore can be seen on this postcard.

Dual Roadways of Garden State Parkway near Atlantic City, New Jersey. Opened in 1954, the Garden State Parkway extends the length of New Jersey, from the New York state line to Cape May, making New Jersey's Southern Shore easily accessible.

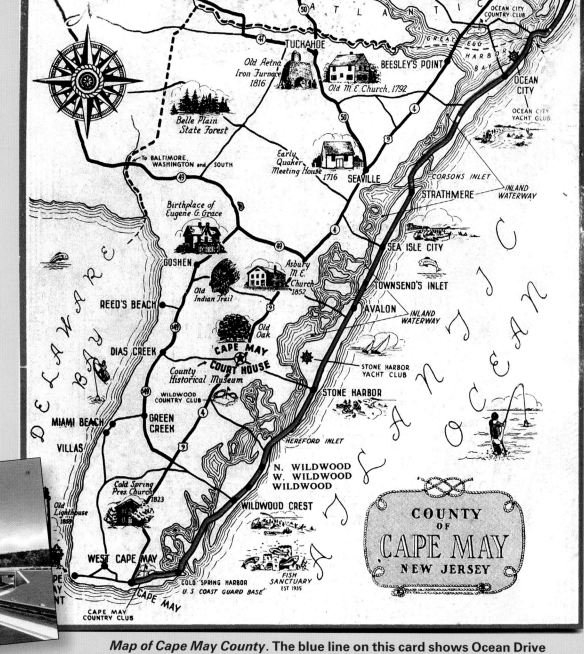

Map of Cape May County. The blue line on this card shows Ocean Drive the, "Scenic Route, 50 Miles Within Sight and Sound of the Ocean."

Greetings from The Jersey Shore. This postcard was sent from New Jersey's Southern Shore to the folks back home. From the back: "Went for a ride on this boat, fishing is great here! Back for work Monday."

Greetings from The Jersey Shore. From the back: "The weather is great, the water is warm, having a great time."

Introduction

The fifteen communities that are commonly known as New Jersey's Southern Shore range from Brigantine – the northernmost island in Atlantic County – to Cape May Point on the southern tip of Cape May County. Each of them is on a barrier island with the bay or inland waterway separating it from the mainland, though each has a bridge that connects it to the neighboring island.

The economy of each of these communities relies, to varying degrees, on summer tourists. Each community is different and attracts different populations. Some are mostly residential while others have boardwalks with amusements and stores selling trinkets and souvenirs. Atlantic City, Ocean City, North Wildwood, and Wildwood, for instance, all have amusement rides, games, restaurants, and stores on their boardwalks. Ventnor City's boardwalk, however, while abutting Atlantic City's, is used only for walking, biking, and quiet enjoyment.

Though some of these communities share an island, each has its own governing body. Atlantic City, Ocean City, and Wildwood have had, since their earliest years, public high schools. The other towns have only elementary schools and the children must travel to neighboring communities to attend high school. In size, these communities vary from tiny Cape May Point at 0.3 square mile to Atlantic City, at 11.92 square miles.

While Atlantic City was built as a place of amusement with the purpose of attracting tourists, Ocean City and Cape May Point were founded as religious resorts: Ocean City by Methodists, Cape May Point by Presbyterians.

However, there is a common denominator that connects the fifteen beach communities of New Jersey's Southern Shore and that is the Atlantic Ocean — with its rolling waves, gently sloping beaches, white sand, and balmy breezes.

My own memories of New Jersey's Southern Shore are many even though I grew up in Washington, D.C. As a child, I spent my summers in the Wildwoods where relatives lived. The boardwalk, with its rides and games of skeeball and pokerino, the wide beach, the shuffleboard court, and the playground by the beach were always my favorite places to go. From Wildwood we would cross the bridge into Cape May to shop and to Cape May Point to look for Cape May diamonds (small quartz stones that have been tumbled smooth by the ocean and are transparent when wet). My family often traveled to Atlantic City for the day to visit my maternal grandparents who summered there. For years, one of my cousins owned a very successful children's store in the heart of Stone Harbor and we often visited there, as well as neighboring Avalon. I still have an aunt and cousins who live in Margate.

My husband, Fred, and I are fortunate to make Ocean City our year-round home. Fred began his career as a lifeguard in Stone Harbor and, later, was a longtime member of the Ocean City Beach Patrol; each summer we go up and down the South Jersey coast for lifeguard races. The beach patrols of the fifteen cities known as New Jersey's Southern Shore compete each summer in inter-city lifeguard races culminating in August with the South Jersey Lifeguard Championship.

Fred and I have been collecting postcards for many years. The postcards in this book range from 1900 to 1960. I hope that these postcard views help bring back your own memories of New Jersey's Southern Shore or introduce you anew to these fifteen beach towns and their histories. Enjoy!

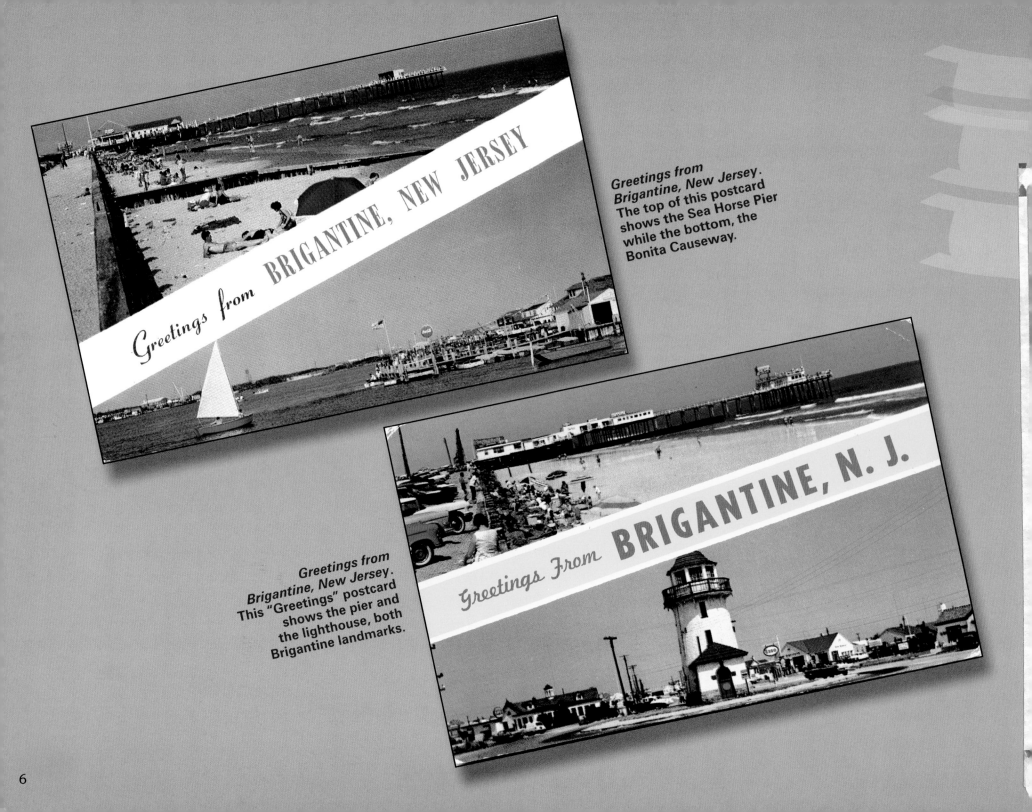

Greetings from Brigantine, New Jersey. The top of this postcard shows the Sea Horse Pier while the bottom, the Bonita Causeway.

Greetings from Brigantine, New Jersey. This "Greetings" postcard shows the pier and the lighthouse, both Brigantine landmarks.

6

Chapter One:
Brigantine

Brigantine, the northernmost city considered part of the South Jersey Shore, is on a barrier island by itself. Its north end is a federally owned shore preserve. The Marine Mammal Stranding Center, dedicated to the rescue and rehabilitation of marine animals, is on Brigantine.

Starting in the late 1800s, attempts were made to develop Brigantine Beach: a railroad was built to connect Philadelphia, Pennsylvania to Brigantine, trolleys ran the length of the island, and hotels were built. By the early 1900s, however, several severe storms had damaged much of the improvements that had been made, and Brigantine fell on hard times.

During the early 1920s the Island Development Company bought most of Brigantine from the Brigantine Land and Transportation Company and again attempted to develop the island. Brigantine was incorporated in 1924. That same year, a bridge between Brigantine and Atlantic City was built and a hotel, houses, a boardwalk, a school, and a golf course soon followed. The crash of the stock market in 1929 and the resulting depression again halted development. The Island Development Company went out of business and deeded its remaining land to the city.

Throughout Brigantine's history, the isolation of the island has been a problem. There are no bridges between Brigantine and the mainland or between Brigantine and the island to its north. Storms have continuously damaged or destroyed the bridge between Brigantine and its southern neighbor, Atlantic City. That isolation, however, became one of the greatest selling points for the development of Brigantine by the late 1940s.

As the population of Atlantic City continued to increase, and with it the price of property, the value of Brigantine, only a mile across the water, was finally recognized. Developers from Philadelphia and New York again began to build and the full time and summer population of Brigantine increased yearly.

Hotel Brigantine, Brigantine Beach, N. J.

Hotel Brigantine, Brigantine Beach, New Jersey.
The Hotel Brigantine opened on June 25, 1927. It was built at a cost of nearly one million dollars and was considered ultra-modern and fireproof.

SEA CHEST APARTMENTS

34th St. at the Ocean, Brigantine, N. J.

86045

Sea Chest Apartments, 34th Street at the Ocean, Brigantine, New Jersey. The ocean front Sea Chest Apartments is described on the back of this card: "Three Rooms with Tile Bath, Modern Kitchen, Double and Twin Beds, Cross Ventilation, Free Parking."

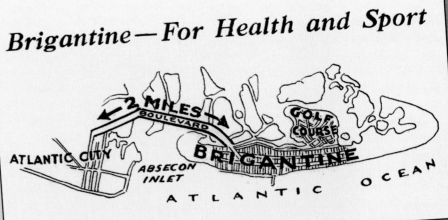

Brigantine — For Health and Sport

ATLANTIC CITY   2 MILES   GOLF COURSE   BRIGANTINE   ABSECON INLET   ATLANTIC OCEAN

Brigantine — For Health and Sport. From the back: "Naturally blessed with a matchless climate and unexcelled facilities for sportsmen, Brigantine holds an additional superiority over all other eastern resorts by reason of its proximity to Atlantic City, the summer amusement capital of America."

It was commonplace to see a U.S. Navy blimp passing over the beach during the 1940s and 1950s.

This replica of a lighthouse was built in 1927 as a real estate sales gimmick. It once housed the town jail.

There were three U.S. Life-Saving Stations on Brigantine Beach. The lifeguards would watch from the towers during the day and patrol the beach at night.

Sand dunes on Brigantine's beach.

This view shows the lifeguards heading out on a rescue.

This postcard shows a breeches buoy
in action during a practice drill.

This is a demonstration of
lifeguards shooting a life-line
in a breeches buoy drill.

Beach Scene at Steel Pier, Atlantic City, N. J.

Beach Scene at Steel Pier, Atlantic City, New Jersey. A crowded beach with cabanas
and beach umbrellas with a view of Steel Pier for the evening's fun.

Chapter Two:
Atlantic City

Atlantic City, just to the south of Brigantine, is on Absecon Island along with Ventnor, Margate, and Longport. Known by the Lenni-Lenape Indians as Absegami as far back as the early 1600s, the island was purchased by a Quaker farmer, Thomas Budd, in 1695. Jeremiah Leeds built a cabin on the island in 1783 and is thought to be the first European to live there. In the early 1850s, Jonathon Pitney, Richard Osborne, and Samuel Richards formed a business partnership to build a railroad from Camden, New Jersey and to develop the island as a tourist destination. Train service began in 1854 and large hotels were immediately built as accommodations. By 1860, Atlantic City had a year-round population of seven hundred and room for up to 4,000 summer visitors. Atlantic City continued to thrive as both a year-round community and a summer destination.

Richard Osborne is said to have chosen the name "Atlantic City," and to have made the decision to name the streets after oceans and states, all of which have become world famous because of the popular board game of Monopoly®.

Atlantic City. This postcard features Atlantic City landmarks, including the bathing beauty!

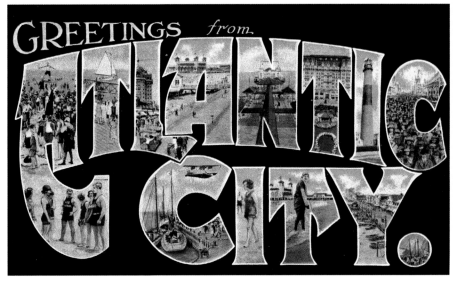

This "Greetings from Atlantic City" postcard shows scenes of the beach, the bay, and the boardwalk.

Bird's-eye View, showing Heinz Pier, Garden Pier, Steel Pier, and Steeple Chase Pier.

Bird's-eye View, showing Heinz Pier, Garden Pier, Steel Pier, and Steeple Chase Pier. **This scene shows four amusement piers**

HEINZ PIER.

Heinz Pier. In 1898, pickle magnate Henry J. Heinz of Pittsburgh bought what had been the Iron Pier for a permanent exhibit of his products. He renamed it Heinz Pier, built sun decks and an enclosed pavilion, and started daily organ concerts. Favorites with visitors were the free pickles and pickle pins given to all patrons.

107 A THRILL OF A MINUTE—DIVING HORSE—OCEAN END STEEL PIER, ATLANTIC CITY, N. J.

3473-29

A Thrill of a Minute – Diving Horse – Ocean End Steel Pier, Atlantic City, New Jersey. **The High Diving Horse was the most famous act in Atlantic City. Bareback riders plunged off of Steel Pier into a pool forty feet below.**

STEEPLECHASE PIER.

Steeplechase Pier opened in 1904. Owned by George C. Tilyou, it was modeled after his pier on Coney Island, New York. It boasted the world's largest electric sign, with 27,000 light bulbs.

14

Garden Pier.

The Garden Pier was an opulent amusement center.

WORLD FAMOUS STEEL PIER

The world famous Steel Pier was Atlantic City's most celebrated entertainment area, often attracting over a million customers a season with acts such as Abbot and Costello, Gypsy Rose Lee, and Bob Hope.

Young's New Million Dollar Pier.

Captain John L. Young opened the Million Dollar Pier in July of 1906. The pier entertained the crowds with vaudeville shows, an aquarium, and other amusements.

Capt. Young's Residence on Million Dollar Pier.

Captain John L. Young built his palatial private residence on his Million Dollar Pier. The address was 1 Atlantic Ocean.

A 1907 postcard of Atlantic City lifeguards: "These are the men who are not afraid of the water."

Sun and Ocean Bathing, Atlantic City, New Jersey. This art deco building is the lifeguard headquarters.

INTERIOR OF HYGEIA SWIMMING POOL, ATLANTIC CITY. N. J.

DANGER   DANGER

The Hygeia Pool was one of several indoor salt water pools that provided "year-'round bathing."

ATLANTIC CITY AUDITORIUM AND CONVENTION HALL, ATLANTIC CITY, N. J.

Atlantic City Auditorium and Convention Hall, Atlantic City, New Jersey.
Convention Hall opened in 1929 at a cost of $13.4 million. At the time, it was the largest building in the world without roof posts. It covered seven acres, including its pavilion on the boardwalk. Known officially as the Atlantic City Auditorium, it is on the National Register of Historic Places.

LARGEST CONVENTION HALL IN THE WORLD, SEATING CAPACITY 40,000, BALL ROOM 5,000

Chelsea Park and High School. In 1923, Atlantic City dedicated a new high school on Albany Avenue. It was said to be the fourth largest school in the world and could accommodate 2,100 students.

Hotel Marlborough-Blenheim from the Beach.
From the back: "The Marlborough-Blenheim Hotel overlooks beautiful Park Place, one of the loveliest small parks on Absecon Island."

Hotel Traymore, Atlantic City, New Jersey. The Traymore Hotel opened its doors in 1915 with six hundred guestrooms and a ballroom that could accommodate 4,000 people. The hotel hosted Presidents Woodrow Wilson, Calvin Coolidge, and Franklin Roosevelt as well as leaders from all walks of life.

Beach Scene at Chalfonete — Hadden Hall Hotels, Atlantic City, N. J. 20N

Beach Scene at Chalfonete — Hadden Hall Hotels, Atlantic City, New Jersey.
From the back: "Facing directly on the Boardwalk in the heart of resort activity, the Chalfonte-Haddon Hall Hotels are known far and wide for their hospitality and comfort."

THE BREAKERS.

The Breakers Hotel was one of several kosher hotels in Atlantic City that catered to Jewish patrons.

World War Memorial. This Memorial was built as a tribute to the veterans of World War I.

The Absecon Lighthouse, on the northern tip of Atlantic City, was built in 1857. The lookout tower of the Atlantic City Life-Saving Station can be seen to the right of the lighthouse. The station was built in 1884.

ATLANTIC CITY
RACE TRACK

The Atlantic City Racetrack was considered one of the most modern tracks in the country where the finest horses, ridden by the finest jockeys, ran.

TERMINUS AT VIRGINIA AVENUE AND BOARDWALK
ATLANTIC CITY

STEEL PIER

Scene along lines of Atlantic City & Shore Railroad, between Atlantic City and Ocean City

Scene along lines of Atlantic City & Shore Railroad, between Atlantic City and Ocean City.
The Atlantic City & Shore Railroad, also known as the Shore Fast Line, was an electric trolley that ran between Atlantic City and Ocean City and through Pleasantville, Northfield, Linwood, and Somers Point on the mainland.

This colorful "Hello from Ventnor City, New Jersey" card lists each of the scenes on its other side.

Greetings from Ventnor City, New Jersey. Fun on the beach!

Chapter Three: Ventnor

In the late 1800s, the Camden and Atlantic Land Company began the development of the area of Absecon Island just south of Atlantic City. In 1889, Mrs. S. Bartram Richards, the wife of the secretary-treasurer of the company, suggested the area be called Ventnor after a town on England's Isle of Wight. In 1891, the company built a five-story, three hundred-room hotel, the Carisbrooke Inn. Ventnor was incorporated as a city from Egg Harbor Township in 1903. The first mayor elected was Alfred C. McClellan, the owner of the Carisbrooke Inn.

Ventnor's first city hall was built in 1907 and housed the police and fire departments as well as city offices. The first school was built in 1911. In 1928, a new city hall, designed by local architect Vivian Smith, was built. Ventnor's boardwalk was erected to connect with Atlantic City's boardwalk, but unlike Atlantic City's, contained no amusement piers, stores, or hotels.

Hello from Ventnor.
From the back: "This beautiful city of homes is situated by the Atlantic Ocean. In the distant background can be seen Atlantic City."

Ventnor, New Jersey. **A view of the Ventnor beach showing a lifeguard boat and the Oxford Apartment building.**

Greetings from Ventnor, New Jersey.
Bathing in the surf is always fun for the family!

159 View from Ventnor Pier, Ventnor City, N. J.

View from Ventnor Pier, Ventnor City, New Jersey.
On the back: "Adjacent to Atlantic City, Ventnor City is a quiet residential section noted for its cleanliness, pure water and recreational facilities."

Ventnor Beach and Boardwalk, Ventnor, N. J.

Ventnor Beach and Boardwalk, Ventnor, New Jersey.
A view of the Ventnor skyline looking north.

A beach scene with the Ventnor Pier in the background.

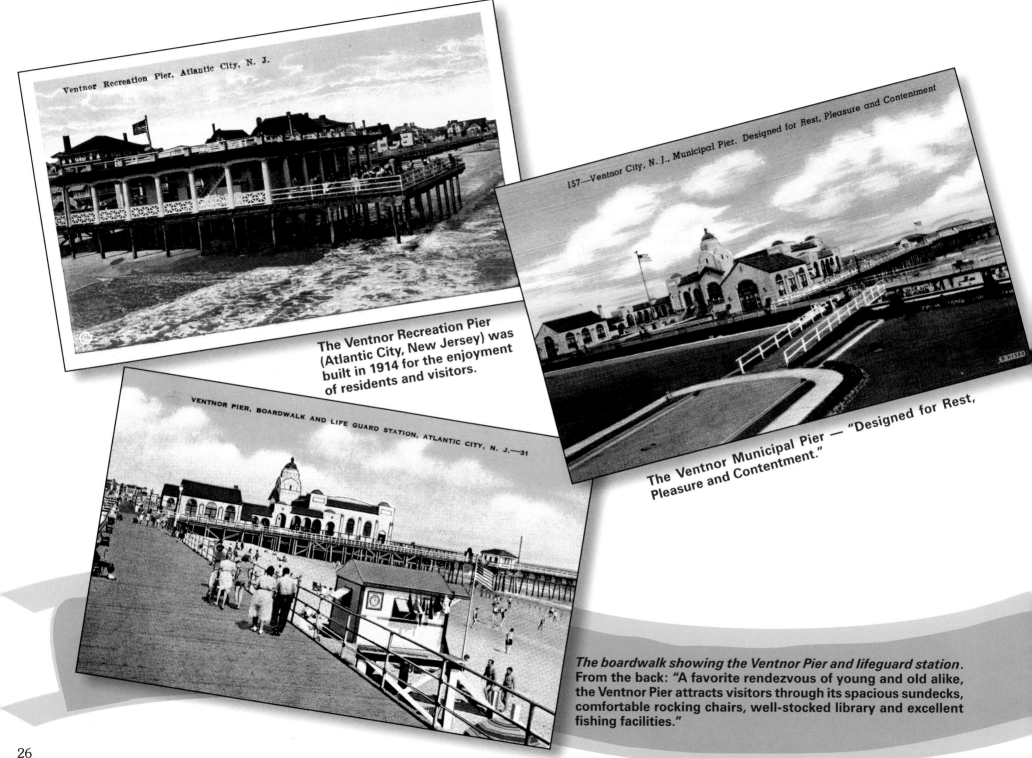

Ventnor Recreation Pier, Atlantic City, N. J.

The Ventnor Recreation Pier (Atlantic City, New Jersey) was built in 1914 for the enjoyment of residents and visitors.

157—Ventnor City, N. J., Municipal Pier. Designed for Rest, Pleasure and Contentment

The Ventnor Municipal Pier — "Designed for Rest, Pleasure and Contentment."

VENTNOR PIER, BOARDWALK AND LIFE GUARD STATION, ATLANTIC CITY, N. J.—31

The boardwalk showing the Ventnor Pier and lifeguard station. From the back: "A favorite rendezvous of young and old alike, the Ventnor Pier attracts visitors through its spacious sundecks, comfortable rocking chairs, well-stocked library and excellent fishing facilities."

Catholic Church, Ventnor, N. J.   V11

Catholic Church, Ventnor, New Jersey.
This church is one of the many churches and synagogues in Ventnor.

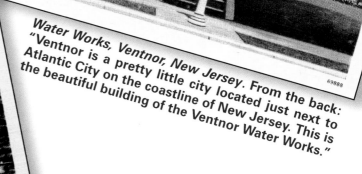

Water Works, Ventnor, N. J.   45

Water Works, Ventnor, New Jersey. From the back:
"Ventnor is a pretty little city located just next to Atlantic City on the coastline of New Jersey. This is the beautiful building of the Ventnor Water Works."

69888

City Hall, Ventnor, N. J.

Ventnor's City Hall was designed in 1928 by local architect Vivian B. Smith in the Jacobean Revival style to evoke the town's namesake in England.

69887

Among The Breakers

A Beautiful Surf Scene

500

GREETINGS FROM MARGATE CITY, N. J.

9 8

Keeping Cool On The Beach

49123

Pleasure Yachting

This "Greetings from Margate" postcard shows four seaside scenes.

Hi from MARGATE CITY

N J

MARGATE CITY

"Hi from Margate City" says it all!

Chapter Four:
Margate

Margate was founded in the mid-1800s as the population of nearby Atlantic City grew. It was called South Atlantic City. In 1881, in an effort to attract real estate buyers to what was then still Egg Harbor Township, Philadelphian James V. Lafferty, Jr, built a six-story hotel and restaurant in the shape of an elephant. He constructed three such buildings, but Margate's, dubbed Lucy the Elephant, is the only one still standing and is now on the National Register of Historic Places.

Lafferty advertised his "Elephant Hotel" in Philadelphia's newspapers and people flocked to the shore to see it. He was so successful in his advertising that, in 1884, the owners of the Camden and Atlantic Railroad continued their tracks down Absecon Island to Margate. In 1892, a trolley system was also extended down the length of the island.

In 1885, the city of South Atlantic City was incorporated as a borough from Egg Harbor Township. On May 3, 1909, South Atlantic City became Margate City, named after the fashionable seaside resort of Margate in England.

Greetings from Margate, New Jersey. This "Greetings" postcard shows the beach and many of the beautiful seagulls that inhabit the area.

The Margate Parkway, Atlantic City, New Jersey.
This is the main road through Margate. With many beautiful homes on its wide street, it is traditionally an area of year-round residents.

Margate Parkway, Margate, N. J.

Margate Parkway, Margate, New Jersey. From the back: "Margate's people live extremely well and enjoy life abundantly. All too few visitors ever realize that the city has many beautiful homes."

77 Margate Parkway, Margate City, N. J.

Margate Parkway, Margate, New Jersey. From the back: "The Margate Parkway is a fairyland of lights during the annual outdoor Christmas Lighting Festival."

7A-H3499

Marvin Gardens, Margate, N. J.

Marvin Gardens, Margate, New Jersey.
This is a distinctive neighborhood of stylish homes. In the game of Monopoly®, Marvin Gardens can be bought for $280.

ELEPHANT HOTEL, MARGATE CITY, AN OLD LANDMARK

THE ONLY ELEPHANT IN THE WORLD YOU CAN GO THROUGH AND COME OUT ALIVE

Elephant Hotel, Margate City, An Old Landmark.
The Elephant Hotel was built in 1881 to attract visitors to the area. "The only elephant in the world you can go through and come out alive."

Elephant Hotel, Margate City, an Old Landmark, Atlantic City, N. J.

Elephant Hotel, Margate City, An Old Landmark, Atlantic City, New Jersey.
Lucy the Elephant is a well known landmark and is on the National Register of Historic Places.

Church of The Blessed Sacrament, Margate City, New Jersey ERECTED 1946

© Copyright   78419

Church of the Blessed Sacrament, Margate City, New Jersey.
Erected in 1946, it's one of several churches and synagogues in Margate.

A Merry Sailing Party.

A Merry Sailing Party.
Sailing off the beautiful Margate beach.

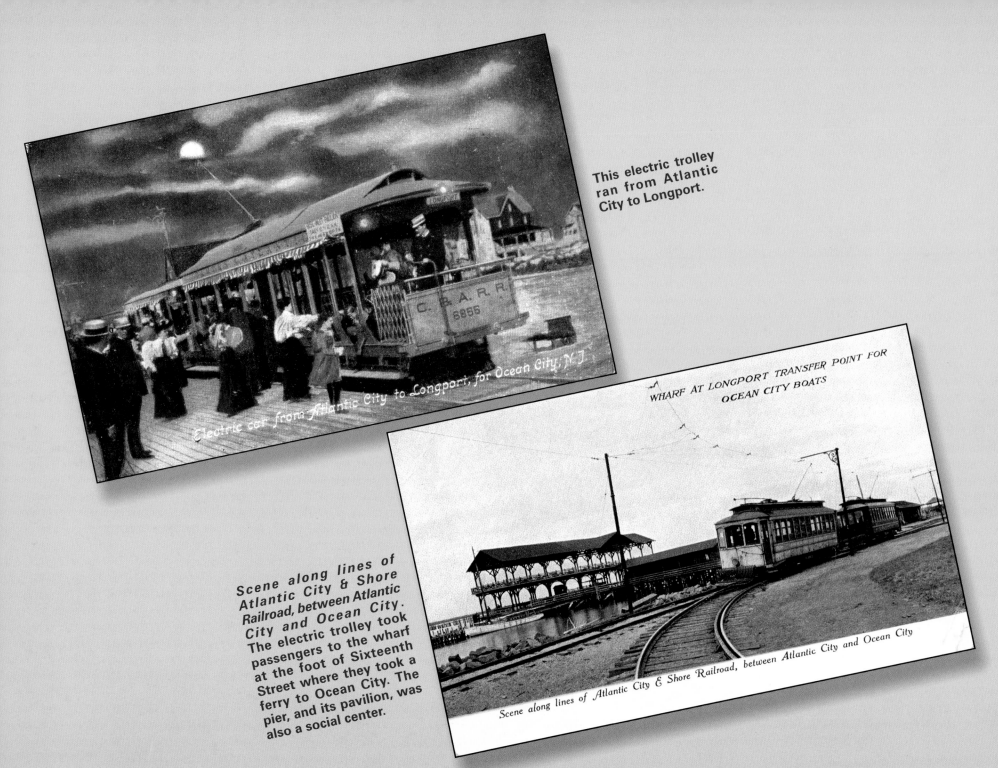

This electric trolley ran from Atlantic City to Longport.

Electric car from Atlantic City to Longport, for Ocean City, N.J.

Scene along lines of Atlantic City & Shore Railroad, between Atlantic City and Ocean City. The electric trolley took passengers to the wharf at the foot of Sixteenth Street where they took a ferry to Ocean City. The pier, and its pavilion, was also a social center.

WHARF AT LONGPORT TRANSFER POINT FOR OCEAN CITY BOATS

Scene along lines of Atlantic City & Shore Railroad, between Atlantic City and Ocean City

A steamer landing at the Longport wharf.

Chapter Five:
Longport

Longport, on the southern end of Absecon Island, is a borough 1.5 miles long and only a half-mile wide. In 1857, James Long bought a portion of land that would later become part of the borough. During the twenty-five years that he owned the land, sand accumulated, adding almost a full mile to his original holding. Long never attempted to develop the land, but sold it to M. Simpson McCullough, who named the area Longport after his friend James Long, and built it into a seashore resort.

The borough of Longport was incorporated in 1898. By 1916, the southern tip of Longport had lost ten of its blocks to sand erosion. This little borough is mostly residential, with only a few commercial properties in its midst.

"The Longport" Boat from Atlantic City for Ocean City, New Jersey. It carried passengers between Longport and Ocean City.

Longport's third U.S. Coast Guard Station was built in 1938. In 1944 it became the Borough Hall.

The John F. Kennedy Memorial Bridge between Longport and Somers Point, on the mainland, was built in 1963 to replace an earlier draw bridge.

Aerial View of Longport, New Jersey. The draw bridge can be seen in this aerial view.

The Devonshire was one of the largest hotels in Longport.

THE ABERDEEN - LONGPORT, N. J.

The Aberdeen Hotel advertised, "As Good as an Ocean Cruise!"

Ocean Bay Apartments, Longport, New Jersey.
From the back: "Modern One and Two Bedroom Efficiency Apartments, Protected Bathing Beach and Fishing Pier, Parking, Television facilities Available, Modern Coffee Shop."

The Ocean Bay Apartments advertised they had a, "Large Swimming Pool and Kiddy Pool."

The Betty Bacharach Home for Afflicted Children, Longport, New Jersey. Founded by Congressman Isaac Bacharach and his brother Harry Bacharach, mayor of Atlantic City, in honor of their mother, "So That They May Walk."

In 1911, Peter Widener built the Widener Industrial School at 29th Street and Atlantic Avenue. Over the years, the building changed hands several times until, in 1949, it was bought by Gospel Hall as a "Home for Aged Christians."

39

The Longport Catholic Church of the Epiphany was dedicated on November 7, 1954.

The Church of the Redeemer, on the corner of 20th Street and Atlantic Avenue, is on the State and National Registers of Historic Places.

The jetty was built at the south end of Longport to stop beach erosion.

171:—THE NEW OCEAN CITY—LONGPORT BRIDGE, OCEAN CITY, N. J.

The New Ocean City— Longport Bridge, Ocean City, New Jersey. The bridge crossing the Great Egg Inlet into Ocean City opened in 1928.

Greetings from Ocean City, New Jersey. This 1930s "Greetings" postcard shows the boardwalk, beach, and bay.

Greetings from Ocean City. This "Greetings" postcard shows many Ocean City landmarks.

Chapter Six:
Ocean City

The City of Ocean City, across the bay from Longport, stands alone on an eight-mile-long island. It is the northernmost community in Cape May County. First known as Peck's Beach, after whaler John Peck, the island was used by mainland farmers to graze their cattle.

Founded in 1879 by Methodist ministers as a Christian Seaside Resort, just twenty-five years after Atlantic City, Ocean City has a very different flavor. A "dry" town, with no bars, liquor stores, or liquor licenses, and where Sunday closings were enforced until 1986, Ocean City bills itself as "America's Greatest Family Resort."

From its inception, Ocean City was planned as a year-round community as well as a summer resort. The founders, ministers Ezra B. Lake, S. Wesley Lake, James E. Lake, William H. Burrell, and William B. Wood, and the Lake brothers' father, Simon Lake, formed the Ocean City Association to conduct the business of the fledgling city. By 1880, they had organized the Pleasantville and Ocean City Railroad, which, along with a steamboat they purchased, would bring people to the island from the mainland. Also in 1880, a newspaper, The Sentinel, began publication and the First Methodist Episcopal Church had been organized. In 1881, the first Post Office opened. A school was started in the Association's offices with the first schoolhouse being built in 1882.

Ocean City was incorporated as a borough from Upper Township in 1884 and was incorporated as a city in 1897.

Hello from Ocean City, New Jersey. **The Ninth Street beach, shown in this view, was the most popular beach with the college crowd.**

Board Walk, Ocean City, New Jersey.
On April 22, 1905, Mayor Joseph G. Champion dedicated the new two-mile long boardwalk saying, "Today we have reached a milestone in our municipal life, marked by the most brilliant event which has ever taken place in the history of the city."

Music Pavilion, Ocean City, N. J.

Music Pavilion, Ocean City, New Jersey.
Built in 1905, it was enlarged a few years later.

Boardwalk and Beach, South from 7th St., Ocean City, N. J.

Boardwalk and Beach, South from 7th Street, Ocean City, New Jersey. Shown in this view, looking south from 7th Street, is Doughty's Pier.

44

Beach and Bathing in Front of Hippodrome, Ocean City, N. J.

Bathing Beach at 10th St. showing Hotel Flanders, Ocean City, N. J.

Beach and Bathing in Front of Hippodrome, Ocean City, New Jersey. The Hippodrome Pier was Ocean City's largest and most popular amusement center before it was destroyed by fire in 1927.

This scene of bathers at 10th Street looks south towards the Hotel Flanders.

Bathing Beach and Boardwalk, Ocean City, New Jersey.
This scene of the 10th Street beach looks north towards the Music Pier.

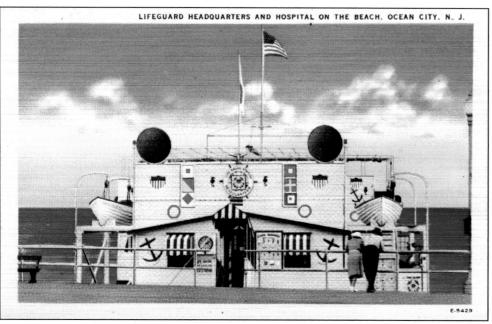

Lifeguard Headquarters and Hospital on the Beach, Ocean City, New Jersey.
The Ocean City Beach Patrol headquarters at 10th Street was one of the finest such buildings in the country.

Municipal Music Pier, Ocean City, New Jersey.
The Music Pier, built in 1928, was the scene of free daily concerts throughout the season.

62993

Bathing Beach and Beach Patrol, Ocean City, N. J.

Bathing Beach and Beach Patrol, Ocean City, New Jersey.
This beach patrol headquarters was built at 1st Street in 1938 because of the increasingly large beach crowds in the north end of the city.

THE BEACH PATROL, OCEAN CITY, N. J.

26619

The Beach Patrol, Ocean City, New Jersey. **The beach patrol lines up in their dress uniforms in front of the Hotel Flanders. Captain Jack Jernee is in the center in white. Note the lifeguard mascot on the right.**

Ocean City Life Guard Boat Races, Ocean City, New Jersey.
The lifeguards hold intra-squad lifeboat races off the 10th Street beach.

U.S. Coast Guard Station, Ocean City, New Jersey.
It was located at 4th Street and Atlantic Avenue.

This U.S. Coast Guard Station was at 36th Street and the beach.

THE "SINDIA"—1901   48

WRECK OF THE "SINDIA" NOW. OCEAN CITY, N. J

This postcard with the "then and now" views of the Sindia was mailed in 1938. The Sindia, a four-masted ship, came ashore between 16th and 17th Streets on December 15, 1901.

301.   U. S. COAST GUARD STATION, NORTH OF 59TH STREET.   OCEAN CITY, N. J.

U.S. Coast Guard Station, north of 59th Street, Ocean City, New Jersey. The station was built as a U.S. Life-Saving Station, as were the 4th Street and 36th Street stations.

EXERCISES ON THE BEACH, OCEAN CITY, N. J.

Exercises on the Beach, Ocean City, New Jersey. Elmer E. Unger, a Lower Merion, Pennsylvania High School physical education teacher, held beach exercises on the 2nd Street beach Monday, Wednesday, and Fridays during the season.

A Crowd on the Boardwalk, Ocean City, New Jersey. This view displays a typical early evening on the boardwalk during the 1930s.

The "Fun Deck" by Moonlight, Ocean City, New Jersey. Gillian's Fun Deck, at Plymouth Place and the Boardwalk, was one of the most popular tourist attractions on the boardwalk.

Ocean City, New Jersey. Playland Amusement Park traces its roots back to Bingham's Kiddie Rides, built in 1939.

Ocean City Yacht Club, Ocean City, New Jersey. It was located at 6th Street and Pleasure Avenue.

14392

Ocean City Yacht Club, Ocean City, New Jersey.
The Yacht Club moved into this building on Battersea Road on August 24, 1912.

This "Greetings from Ocean City" postcard shows four churches. Religion has always been an important part of the community.

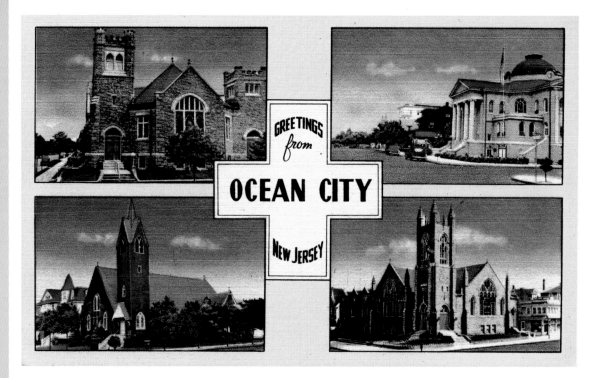

Tabernacle and Camp Meeting Grounds, Ocean City, New Jersey. The Tabernacle Auditorium opened in 1881 on the Camp Meeting Grounds between 5th and 6th Streets.

225   Tabernacle and Camp Meeting Grounds, Ocean City, N. J.

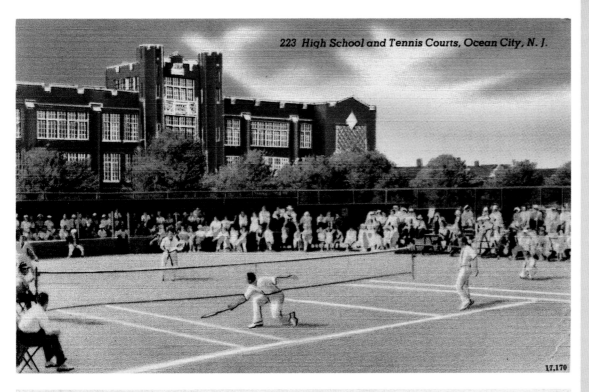

223 *High School and Tennis Courts, Ocean City, N. J.*

17,170

High School and Tennis Courts, Ocean City, New Jersey. The tennis courts in front of the new high school were used by the community as well as the students.

SHUFFLE-BOARD COURTS ON THE BEACH FRONT, OCEAN CITY, NEW JERSEY

TENNIS COURTS BETWEEN 5TH AND 6TH ST., OCEAN CITY, N. J.   49559

Shuffle-board and tennis have always been popular sports in Ocean City.

HOTEL FLANDERS AND OUTDOOR POOLS, OCEAN CITY, N. J.

The Hotel Flanders, the largest hotel in Ocean City, had a large pool, a diving pool, and a children's pool.

Hotel Normandie, Ocean City, N. J.

Hotel Normandie, Ocean City, New Jersey. The Normandie Hotel, at the corner of 9th Street and Ocean Avenue, was the second largest hotel in town. It was destroyed by fire on October 11, 1927.

The Hotel Delaware, on the Boardwalk at 3rd Street, was built in 1925.

Hotel Biscayne, Ocean City, New Jersey. Located at 812 Ocean Avenue, it was where New Jersey Governor Woodrow Wilson stayed when he came to Ocean City September 28, 1911.

In 1958, the Seaspray Motel, located at 34th Street and Bay Avenue, advertised that it was "Ocean City's First and Finest Motel."

Strathmere – P & R Excursion. The Pennsylvania and Reading Excursion train ran between Ocean City, Strathmere, and Sea Isle City.

STRATHMERE P&R EXCURSION.

U.S. Coast Guard Station, Strathmere, New Jersey.
This U.S. Coast Guard Station was moved from the south end of Ocean City across Corson's Inlet to Strathmere in 1924. It was built as a U.S. Life-Saving Station in Ocean City in 1899.

U. S. COAST GUARD STATION, STRATHMERE, N. J.

Chapter Seven:
Strathmere

Continuing south, and sharing an island with Sea Isle City, is Strathmere, first known as Corson's Inlet after John and Peter Corson, who had sailed across the inlet between what would become Ocean City and Strathmere. Around 1881, the island was deeded to Mathilda Landis, who, along with Charles Landis and the Sea Isle City Improvement Corporation, helped develop the island. In 1884, tracks for the West Jersey Railroad were laid up the coast from Cape May through Corson's Inlet to Ocean City, making it easier to get to the island. Several hotels and cottages were built.

In 1905, the town of Corson's Inlet was annexed to Upper Township. In 1908, the Atlantic Seashore Improvement Company of Pennsylvania began to develop the community and in 1912 changed the name to Strathmere. The town is 1.5 miles long and only two blocks wide.

STRATHMERE
"BY-THE-SEA"

Strathmere "By-The-Sea." **This promotional postcard declared, from the back: "Unexcelled Bathing-Fishing-Sailing-Crabbing, Ocean City (Across the Inlet), 60 Miles from Philadelphia, 8 Miles from Atlantic City, Excellent Train Service."**

Bathing Beach, Strathmere, New Jersey. The lifeguards assured the safety of the bathers.

BATHING BEACH, STRATHMERE, N.J.

This aerial view of Strathmere looks from the bay towards the ocean.

STRATHMERE, N. J., LOOKING FROM THE BAY TOWARDS THE OCEAN

THE SPOILS OF A DAYS SPORT WITH THE ROD IN THE WATERS OFF STRATHMERE, N. J.

Fishing was a favorite activity in the waters off Strathmere.

A View of Corson's Inlet, N. J. from R. R. Bridge.

View of Corson's Inlet, New Jersey from the railroad bridge. The Whelen Hotel, built in 1871, can be seen in the background. The Whelen later became the Deauville Inn.

"Strathmere Shines as Fishing Resort" proclaims this 1933 promotional postcard.

$795 TYPE BUNGALOW AT STRATHMERE, N. J.

2 miles from Ocean City. Including lot 30 x 100. 4 rooms and porch. Size 18 ft. x 26 ft.

The Ideal Family Resort—Wonderful Surf Bathing—Smooth, Gently Sloping Beach—

Untainted, Energizing Sunshine—Pure Iodine-laden Salt Air—Every Modern Convenience

GIRARD BROS., S. E. Cor. 7th & Federal Sts., Philadelphia

This bungalow was available for only $795, including a 30 X 100 foot lot, according to this 1933 postcard ad.

S.W. COR. PUTNAM + COMMONWEALTH AVE.
STRATHMERE " BY THE SEA "

The Bayview Motel and Apartments had sixty-five rooms with bath and advertised that it was, "Strathmere's Finest."

This bungalow was on the corner of Putnam and Commonwealth Avenue.

Greetings From
SEA ISLE CITY
NEW JERSEY
K8347

This "Greetings from Sea Isle City" postcard shows scenes of the beach, the bay, and the boardwalk.

Another "Greetings from Sea Isle City" postcard. Circa 1950s.

greetings from SEA ISLE CITY, N.J.

Beach Scene from Boardwalk, Sea Isle City, New Jersey. This scene shows a crowded beach with the lifeguards keeping a close eye on the bathers.

Chapter Eight:
Sea Isle City

Sea Isle City was originally called Ludlam's Beach after Joseph Ludlam, who had purchased the island in 1692 and used it for cattle and sheep grazing. In 1879 Charles Landis bought the island with the intention of developing a city to rival Venice, Italy, including its canals. By 1882, a railroad line ran across the marshes to Ludlam's Beach, allowing easier travel from the mainland, and Landis and his partners had built an excursion house and ten cottages for visitors. They also installed gas lines, electricity, and waterworks.

In 1882 residents voted to incorporate as the borough of Sea Isle City, severing ties with Dennis Township. The first mayor elected was Martin Wells. The federal government built the Ludlam's Beach Lighthouse in 1885. Townsend's Inlet, as the southernmost part of Sea Isle City is called, is named after John Townsend, who purchased that part of the island from Joseph Ludlam in 1695. It is known as the best fishing grounds along the New Jersey coast.

Boardwalk and Beach at 41st Street, Sea Isle City, New Jersey. A typical beach scene with a view of buildings on the boardwalk at 41st Street.

Ocean Pier, Sea Isle City, New Jersey — a place for rest and recreation.

Ocean Pier at Sea Isle City, New Jersey.
From the Ocean Pier, one had a good view of the beach

Boardwalk and Concert Stand, Sea Isle City, New Jersey. The concert stand was a very popular boardwalk attraction.

Watching the Baby Parade, Sea Isle City, New Jersey. The Baby Parade, held on the boardwalk, always drew a crowd of spectators.

Boardwalk, Sea Isle City, New Jersey. The Sea Isle City Amusement Parlor was a popular place with young people.

44th Street Bridge, Sea Isle City, N. J.

68145

44th Street Bridge, Sea Isle City, New Jersey.
The drawbridge at 44th Street was replaced in 1964 with a fixed span bridge.

MEMORIAL PARK, SEA ISLE CITY, N. J.

Memorial Park, Sea Isle City, New Jersey is at 41st Street and Landis Avenue.

LANDIS AVENUE, LOOKING NORTH FROM 43RD STREET, SEA ISLE CITY, N. J

U. S. POST OFFICE ON RIGHT.

"Landis Avenue, Looking North from 43rd Street."

Landis Ave. North from North 41st Street Showing Cronecker's Hotel and Cafe, Sea Isle City, N. J.

This view of Landis Avenue, looking north from 41st Street, shows Cronecker's Hotel and Café.

CRONECKER'S HOTEL, SEA ISLE CITY, N. J.

Cronecker's Hotel, Sea Isle City, New Jersey — it advertised in 1951 that they served, "America's Finest Foods and Liquors Since 1887."

Surf House, Sea Isle City, New Jersey — it was one of the first hotels built in Sea Isle City.

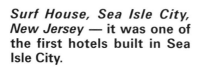

Surf House, Sea Isle City, N. J.

8. COLONNADE HOTEL, SEA ISLE CITY, N. J.

Colonnade Hotel, Sea Isle City, New Jersey. Located at 46th Street and Landis Avenue, the hotel was close to the beach.

12. DEPOT HOTEL, SEA ISLE CITY, N. J.

Depot Hotel, Sea Isle City, New Jersey — it was built near the railroad station.

13. PENN. RAILROAD STATION, SEA ISLE CITY, N. J.

*Pennsylvania Railroad Station,
Sea Isle City, New Jersey.*
**The train offered special
weekend excursion rates.**

CITY HALL, SEA ISLE CITY, N. J.

*City Hall, Sea Isle City,
New Jersey.*
**Located at 44th Street
and Landis Avenue, it is
where all city business
was enacted.**

SEA ISLE CITY HOSPITAL, SEA ISLE CITY, N. J.

Sea Isle City Hospital, at 48th Street and Pleasure Avenue, was established in 1926 for the care of mentally disabled children.

PUBLIC SCHOOL, SEA ISLE CITY, N. J.

Public School, Sea Isle City, New Jersey.
Sea Isle City students attended this school through the eighth grade, but had to travel to Ocean City for high school.

New Club House, Sea Isle Yacht and Motor Club, Sea Isle City. The Sea Isle City Yacht Club held a series of sailing races each summer. It was also the setting of many social activities during the season.

This *Fishing Crew* was one of many who fished in the waters off Sea Isle City.

Light House, Sea Isle City, New Jersey. Ludlam's Beach Lighthouse, at 31st Street and the beach, was built in 1885.

The Beach Patrol, Sea Isle City, N. J.

The Beach Patrol, Sea Isle City. Sea Isle City Beach Patrol Captain Antonio "Jumbo" Cannova and his lifeguards stand in front of their headquarters in 1930. In the early days of lifeguarding, headquarters were tents that could be removed from the beach at the end of the season.

Life Saving Station at Sea Isle City, N. J.

This *Life-Saving Station* was built in 1888 as part of the U.S. Life-Saving Service.

LIFE GUARD, SEA ISLE CITY, N. J.

Life Guard, Sea Isle City, New Jersey. In this later picture (after 1930) of Sea Isle City Beach Patrol Captain Cannova and his lifeguards, their headquarters is now a wooden building.

BEACH AND SURF VIEW

HELLO FROM **TOWNSENDS INLET** NEW JERSEY

Hello from Townsends Inlet, New Jersey.
This "Beach and Surf View" is from Townsend's Inlet, another name for the south end of Sea Isle City.

U. S. Life Saving Station, Townsends Inlet, N. J.

This U.S. Life-Saving Station was built in Townsend's Inlet in 1886.

Busch Hotel, Sea Isle City, New Jersey. Busch's Hotel and Restaurant, at 87th Street and Landis Avenue, specialized in lobsters and soft shelled crabs.

Busch Hotel, Sea Isle City, N. J.

BUSCH

SCHEMM'S BEER.

INLET HOTEL.

Townsend's Inlet, Sea Isle City, New Jersey. The Inlet Hotel, on the bay in the far south end of Sea Isle City, was advertised as being, "ideal for boating, fishing and gunning."

TOWNSEND'S INLET, SEA ISLE CITY, N.J.

This "Greetings from Avalon" postcard features scenes of the beach.

Coastal Highway Bridge, Avalon, New Jersey. This bridge, one of the coastal highway bridges that link the barrier islands, connects Avalon to Sea Isle City.

Chapter Nine:
Avalon

Avalon, the beach community across Townsend's Inlet from Sea Isle, is located on part of Seven Mile Island. In 1722, Aaron Leaming bought Seven Mile Island for $380 from its British owner. At the time, and for years afterwards, it was only used to graze cattle, to hunt, and to beach whales. It was known as Leaming's Beach. The Tatham Family purchased the island from the Leamings in the early 1800s and built the first permanent structures: beach houses to be used by excursionists who visited the island.

This aerial view of Avalon looks from the bay to the ocean.

In 1887 the Seven Mile Beach Company purchased the island, built a hotel, and sold large tracts of land to other developers. Two years later the company gave the West Jersey Railroad the right to build rail lines from the mainland across to, and the length of, the island, and development really took off. In 1888, a Post Office was established in Avalon. That same year, the Peermont Land Corporation bought six hundred acres and developed it as a seaside resort. For many years, Avalon and Peermont were two separate communities; each had a school, a post office, and a fire department. There was also a small strip of land just north of what would become Stone Harbor, known as Holiday Beach. This small area had its own railroad station. Gradually, Holiday Beach, Peermont, and Avalon merged.

Avalon incorporated as a borough in 1891, separating from Middle Township. The Avalon Beach Development Corporation bought the island in 1907 with the intention of making it into "The Jewel of the Jersey Coast." The corporation built a boardwalk in the early 1900s and, in 1912, the first school opened.

In 1911, a bridge over the Inland Waterway between Avalon and the mainland was built. By 1933, the cost of maintaining the train bridge over Townsend's Inlet had become prohibitive and the railroad discontinued service into Avalon; the trains, which had played such an important role in the development of Avalon, were replaced by buses. As automobiles became prevalent, the interest in Avalon as both a summer resort and a year-round community continued to grow

Broadwalk and Beach at 21st St., Avalon, N. J.

34

7-3140

Boardwalk and Beach at 21st Street, Avalon. The lifeguard headquarters was at 21st Street and the beach

Avalon Pier at Night, Avalon, N. J.

39

82578

Avalon Pier at Night. The Avalon Pier was built in 1929 at 29th Street and the boardwalk.

Bathing Beach Avalon, N. J.

65584

Bathing Beach, Avalon, New Jersey. Avalon boasted some of the widest beaches on the southern coast.

This U.S. Life-Saving Station was built in 1894.

"Cottages Along Princeton
Harbor, Avalon, New Jersey."

Fishing is a favorite pastime for many visitors. This postcard says it all for the busy fisherman.

The Avalon Hotel, at 7th Street and First Avenue: "Where the Ocean Meets the Bay."

Greetings from Avalon, New Jersey.
The Avalon Yacht Club opened in 1941 and soon became the focal point of Avalon's summer social scene.

Greetings from Avalon, New Jersey.
One of the many beautiful lagoons is shown in this view.

Puritan Hotel, Avalon, N. J.

Puriton Hotel, Avalon. Located at 20th Street and the beach, was one of the earliest hotels.

Princeton Hotel & Grille, Avalon, N.J.

Sacred Heart Roman Catholic Church, Avalon, N.J.

Sacred Heart Roman Catholic Church, Avalon. Located at First Avenue and 25th Street, it was completed in 1928.

PRINCETON GRILLE

Princeton Hotel & Grille, Avalon, New Jersey. The Princeton Hotel was another of the early hotels.

MOONLIGHT TINTS THE SURF WITH SILVER
AVALON, N. J.

"Moonlight Tints the Surf with Silver." Moonlight on the surf always makes a lovely postcard.

A "Greetings from Stone Harbor" postcard with a view of the beach in the background.

Greetings from Stone Harbor, New Jersey. This "Greetings" postcard has a view of the yacht club as well as the beach and ocean.

BATHING BEACH AT 96TH STREET, STONE HARBOR, N. J.

Bathing Beach at 96th Street, Stone Harbor. **This view of the beach at 96th Street showing the lifeguard headquarters was postmarked 1939.**

Chapter Ten:
Stone Harbor

Although Stone Harbor shares Seven Mile Island with Avalon, its development came a little later. It was named after an English sea captain named Stone, who had found a safe place to anchor from a severe storm in a natural harbor behind the island. The area changed hands several times until the Stone Harbor Improvement Corporation bought it in 1891. By 1893 they had built a hotel and several houses. A post office was established in 1894. Access to Stone Harbor, however, was difficult; as late as 1910, the train from Avalon was the only means into the town.

In 1905, Stone Harbor was bought at a sheriff's sale by the South Jersey Realty Company, which was owned by brothers Howard, David, and Reese Risley. They proceeded to lay out the area in a geometric pattern with streets running east and west and avenues running north and south. In 1911 a highway to the mainland, including two bridges that stretched over the island's waterways, was built. In 1912, the first schoolhouse was built, a lifeguard was hired to patrol the beach, the first policeman was hired, with the title of "Watchman," and the Stone Harbor Volunteer Fire Department was formed. In 1914, Stone Harbor was incorporated as a borough, with a mayor-council form of government.

The U.S. Life-Saving Station in Stone Harbor was built in 1895 at the south end of the island. In 1948, the American Legion Post 331 purchased the building from the government.

From the back: "Beauty takes over at Stone Harbor, NJ. Truly the Seashore at its best."

Stone Harbor Beach Patrol. This postcard shows the 1960 Stone Harbor Beach Patrol. The author's husband, Fred, is second from left in front row.

2nd Avenue Boulevard looking North, Stone Harbor, N. J. *241*

"Second Avenue
Boulevard looking
North, Stone Harbor,
New Jersey."

2nd Ave. Boulevard, looking South, Stone Harbor, N. J.

"Second Avenue
Boulevard looking
South, Stone Harbor,
New Jersey."

212

Looking West on 96th Street, Stone Harbor, N. J.

"Looking West on 96th Street, Stone Harbor, New Jersey."

Birdseye View 96th Street, Stone Harbor, N. J.

Birdseye View, 96th Street, Stone Harbor, New Jersey. **This 96th Street view, looking towards the ocean, shows the water tower.**

Harbor Theatre at Night, Stone Harbor, N. J.

Harbor Theatre at Night, Stone Harbor, New Jersey. The Harbor Theater at 96th Street opened in 1949. It could seat eight hundred people.

Villa Maria by the Sea, Stone Harbor, N. J.

Villa Maria by the Sea, Stone Harbor, New Jersey. This Convent, at 111th Street, was built circa 1937 as a summer retreat for Sister Servants of the Immaculate Heart of Mary. It is the largest building in Stone Harbor.

2nd Ave & Water Works, Stone Harbor, N, J.

2nd Avenue & Water Works, Stone Harbor, New Jersey. The Water Works building at 2nd Avenue and 96th Street was built in 1924.

The Borough Hall at 95th Street and Second Avenue was completed in 1956.

On August 3, 1912, the first air mail delivery in New Jersey took place between Stone Harbor and Ocean City.

This bungalow colony, between 108th and 111th Streets off 3rd Avenue, was built between 1915 and 1917.

The Bird Sanctuary at the south end of Stone Harbor was founded in 1947. Thousands of birds nest there during the spring and summer.

Scene in 96th Street Basin at Stone Harbor, N. J.

Scene in 96th Street Basin at Stone Harbor.
In this view of the 96th Street lagoon, the children seem to be enjoying themselves off the floating dock.

12190

New Coastal Highway Bridge Between Stone Harbor and Wildwood-By-The-Sea.
This bridge between Stone Harbor and North Wildwood, over Hereford Inlet, is part of Ocean Drive.

This "Greetings from North Wildwood" postcard shows scenes of the beach, ocean, and Wildwood Catholic High School.

The Hereford Inlet Lighthouse, at the northern end of North Wildwood, began operation in 1874.

Chapter Eleven:
The Wildwoods

North Wildwood, Wildwood, and Wildwood Crest

North Wildwood, Wildwood, and Wildwood Crest share the island of Five Mile Beach and are known collectively as the Wildwoods.

NORTH WILDWOOD

North Wildwood, first known as Anglesea, was settled by Scandinavian fishermen who established a fishing village near Hereford Inlet at the northern tip of Five Mile Beach during the mid 1800s. The Hereford Inlet Lighthouse was built in 1874.

In 1882, real estate developer Frederick Swope and his Five Mile Beach Improvement Company bought Anglesea from Humphrey Cresse and began building summer cottages. He also built the Anglesea Railroad to connect with the West Jersey Railroad and the mainland to help bring people onto the island. The village was incorporated as a borough in 1885. In 1898, Henry Ottens began the building boom that transformed Anglesea from a small community to a major seaside resort. He built a large hotel and made improvements to the harbor. In 1906 Anglesea became the borough of North Wildwood and in 1917 the resort was incorporated as a city.

AIRPLANE VIEW OF WILDWOOD-BY-THE-SEA, N. J. 67

Airplane View of Wildwood-By-The-Sea, New Jersey. **This aerial view looks towards Hereford Inlet.**

U. S. Life Saving Station, Anglesea, N. J.

U.S. Life-Saving Station, Anglesea, New Jersey. **It was built in 1888 near the Hereford Inlet Lighthouse.**

FISHING BOATS AT ANGLESEA, N. J.

Fishing Boats at Anglesea, New Jersey.
Fishing has always been important at the shore.

Surfside Hotel, at 25th Avenue and Boardwalk, North Wildwood, N. J.

The Surfside Hotel was at 25th Avenue and the Boardwalk.

96:—NORTH WILDWOOD BOARDWALK BY NIGHT SHOWING SURFSIDE HOTEL, WILDWOOD, N. J.

30619

North Wildwood Boardwalk by Night.
This boardwalk scene at night features the game of skeeball, a show, and the Surfside Hotel.

100:—Bathing at Sportland Looking towards Fishing Pier, North Wildwood, N. J.

Bathing at Sportland, Looking towards Fishing Pier, North Wildwood.
This beach scene looks towards the fishing pier.

Central Avenue looking North from 26th Ave., Wildwood-by-the-Sea, N. J.

Central Avenue, looking north from 26th Avenue, Wildwood-by-the-Sea.
This view shows the large homes in the area.

3 SPORTLAND ON THE BOARDWALK AT WILDWOOD-BY-THE-SEA, N. J.   121083

Sportland on the Boardwalk at Wildwood-By-The-Sea.
The Sportland Pool had water follies and other water-related amusements.

**Ed Zaberer opened his first restaurant in North Wildwood in 1954.
He went on to build the largest restaurant in the Wildwoods,
able to serve 4,000 people in twelve dining rooms.**

Manor Hotel, Wildwood-by-the-Sea, N. J.   208

17,160

Manor Hotel, Wildwood-By-The-Sea, New Jersey.
The Manor Hotel, at 24th and Surf Avenues, was the largest hotel in North Wildwood when it opened in 1907.

North Wildwood Arch, Wildwood, N. J., showing Hotel Cromwell on the right, Hotel Pennsylvania on the left

NORTH WILDWOOD

60-174

North Wildwood Arch, Wildwood, New Jersey, showing the Cromwell Hotel on the right and the Pennsylvania Hotel on the left. This cement arch, built in 1911, was at 26th Street and Atlantic Avenue and marked the entrance to North Wildwood from Wildwood.

"Greetings from Wildwood By The Sea."

Greetings from Wildwood By The Sea. Another "Greetings" card showing scenes of the beach and boardwalk.

"Hello from Wildwood, New Jersey."

Wildwood

Wildwood, or Wildwood-By-The-Sea as it is often called, began as two separate communities: Holly Beach and Wildwood. Holly Beach, the area just south of North Wildwood, was named for its abundance of holly trees. It was developed first, beginning in 1882 when John Burk formed the Holly Beach Improvement Company. The company bought large tracts of land for development and aggressively marketed it as a resort area. During the 1880s, Holly Beach was the fastest growing of the communities on Five Mile Beach.

Wildwood, which was the area just south of Holly Beach, was developed in the mid 1880s mainly through the efforts of brothers Phillip, Latimer, and J. Thompson Baker. Phillip had been an original investor in both Sea Isle City and Holly Beach. The brothers formed the Wildwood Beach Improvement Company and called the area "Wildwood" because the area was so heavily wooded. In 1895 the Borough of Wildwood was incorporated. By 1899, the company had built hotels, cottages, and the first boardwalk. The boardwalk, with restaurants and amusement rides, quickly became popular and was a big draw for Wildwood. The two communities, the borough of Holly Beach and the borough of Wildwood, were consolidated into the City of Wildwood in 1912.

"Manning the Lifeboat" and "Listening to the Band on Wildwood's Boardwalk."

Listening to the Band on Wildwood's Boardwalk N.J.

Manning the Life Boat.

U.S. Life Saving Station, Pacific & Leaming Ave. City of Wildwood, N. J.

U.S. Life-Saving Station, Pacific & Learning Avenues, City of Wildwood. **It was built in 1899.**

BOARDWALK, HOLLY BEACH, N. J.

Boardwalk, Holly Beach, New Jersey. Holly Beach merged with Wildwood in 1912.

W-27—Beach Health Classes, Wildwood-by-the-Sea, N. J.

Beach Health Classes, Wildwood-by-the-Sea, New Jersey. Exercise classes were held on the Wildwood beach.

The Famous Annual Baby Parade, Wildwood, N. J.

ARCADE WAY TO BOARDWALK

BOWLING

60-109

Wildwood's Baby Parade was always a big summer event.

General View along the Boardwalk, Wildwood-By-The-Sea, N. J.

W117

MANCHESTER ART GALLE
AUCTION
3415 AUCTION

14418

General View along the Boardwalk, Wildwood-By-The-Sea, New Jersey.
The boardwalk is always a busy place.

Boardwalk North from Cedar Ave., Wildwood-by-the-Sea, N. J.

DANCING
23 FLAVORS
AMUSEMENTS
TAUBERS
THE SIGHTSEEN

Boardwalk, North from Cedar Avenue, Wildwood-By-The-Sea, New Jersey.
"Watch the tram car, please," is the refrain heard on the Wildwood boardwalk as the little yellow cars go by. The tram cars carry passengers up and down the boardwalk.

BOARDWALK AT REGENT THEATRE, WILDWOOD, N. J.

Boardwalk at Regent Theatre, Wildwood. A view of the boardwalk and beach looking north showing the popular Regent Theatre.

The author's sister Joanie, left, her cousin Susan, middle, and the author pose in the ocean on the Wildwood beach during the 1950s.

Playland, Wildwood-by-the-Sea, N. J.

Playland, Wildwood-by-the-Sea, New Jersey. Playland Amusements was the setting for the famous Caterpillar ride.

Boardwalk and Hunts Starlight Ballroom, Wildwood by the Sea, N. J.

The boardwalk and Hunts Starlight Ballroom, Wildwood-by-the-Sea. Dick Clark's American Bandstand was broadcast from the Starlight.

TENNIS COURTS AND BOARDWALK AT FOX PARK WILDWOOD, N. J.   61

Tennis Courts and Boardwalk at Fox Park, Wildwood. Public tennis courts were just off the boardwalk.

W-30—Shuffleboard Courts, Wildwood-by-the-Sea, N. J.
Sun Deck and Sun Dial Apartments and Hotel Oceanic in Background

A view of the shuffleboard courts shows the Sun Dial Apartments and Hotel Oceanic in the background.

SB-H188

ATLANTIC AVE., LOOKING SOUTH FROM PINE AVE., WILDWOOD BY THE SEA, N. J. 107

Atlantic Avenue looking south from Pine Avenue, Wildwood-by-the-Sea. The Hotel Davis and Hotel Drayton are shown.

W-8—United States Post Office
Wildwood By-the-Sea, N. J.

United States Post Office, Wildwood-by-the-Sea. On Memorial Day, 1936, Congressman Isaac Bacharach, Mayor Doris W. Bradway, and Postmaster Shortt laid the cornerstone for the new U.S. Post Office at 3311 Atlantic Avenue.

HIGH SCHOOL, WILDWOOD, N. J.

Wildwood High School is at Baker and Pacific Avenues.

P. R. R. Depot, Wildwood, N. J.

The Pennsylvania Railroad Station. Trains played an important part in the development of Wildwood.

Commercial Fishing Fleet in Otten's Harbor, Wildwood-by-the-Sea, N. J.

Commercial Fishing Fleet in Otten's Harbor, Wildwood-by-the-Sea.
Otten's Harbor is named after the Otten family. Henry Otten was instrumental in the development of North Wildwood.

W-49

PACIFIC AVENUE AND ASTOR ROAD

"THE ATLANTA", SEAVIEW AND LAVENDER ROADS

Greetings from Wildwood Crest, N. J.

AMUSEMENT CENTER

BATHING BEACH AND FISHING PIER

7A-H2320

This "Greetings from Wildwood Crest" postcard highlights things to see and do.

Greetings from **WILDWOOD CREST, N. J.**

This "Greetings from Wildwood Crest" postcard highlights the beach.

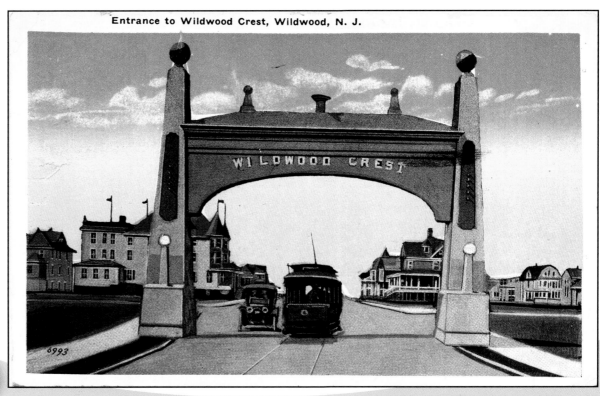

6993

Wildwood Crest

Entrance to Wildwood Crest, Wildwood, New Jersey.
This cement arch was built in 1907 and spanned Pacific Avenue at Cresse Avenue to mark the entrance from Wildwood into Wildwood Crest.

Wildwood Crest owes its development to Phillip, Latimer, and J. Thompson Baker. The area, first purchased in 1717 from George I of England by Thomas Swain, was bought in 1886 by the Bakers, who immediately started developing it along with the area that would become Wildwood. By 1906, the Bakers had built their first houses. Also that year, the first baby was born there: Baker Crest Thurber. The Bakers deeded him his own lot.

In 1910, the area was incorporated as the borough of Wildwood Crest. Phillip Baker was elected mayor. Wildwood Crest consisted of an eighteen-block development with homes, hotels, boarding houses, and Crest Pier, the entertainment center of the town. Nearly all of Wildwood Crest was planned residential, with only a small area in the town center for commercial endeavors.

The beach at Wildwood Crest, because of the topography of the island, gained more and more sand each year. In 1910 the street bordering the ocean was called Atlantic Avenue, but by the 1920s the beach had gained so much sand that Atlantic Avenue was moved closer to the ocean; the old Atlantic Avenue became Seaview Avenue.

CREST PIER, BATHING BEACH AND SEWARD APARTMENTS, WILDWOOD CREST, N. J.

This view of the beach shows the Crest Pier on the left and the Seward Apartments on the right.

Ocean Pier,
Wildwood Crest, N. J.

Ocean Pier, Wildwood Crest, New Jersey.
Built in 1906, the Crest Amusement Pier had bowling alleys, an eight hundred seat theater, a dancing pavilion, a roller skating rink, and a bath house. It was destroyed by fire in 1917.

Crest Pier, at Night Wildwood Crest, N. J.

W-50—Crest Beach and Fishing Pier Looking South from Cresse Ave., Wildwood Crest, N. J.

"The Beach and Fishing Pier Looking South from Cresse Avenue."

The Ocean Front at the Breakers Hotel, Wildwood Crest, N. J.

Crest Pier, at Night. The new Crest Pier opened in May of 1921. It offered a billiards hall, a movie theater, a confectioner, and a combination auditorium and dance hall.

The Ocean front at the Breakers Hotel, Wildwood Crest, New Jersey. Pictured is the pavilion of the Breakers Hotel, Orchid Road, and the beach. The hotel was open only during the summer season.

111

Crest Fishing Pier, Wildwood Crest, N. J.

Crest Fishing Pier, Wildwood Crest, New Jersey. Fishing off the Pier was a favorite activity for many.

The Pelham Hotel
at Lavender Road,
Wildwood Crest,
New Jersey.

THE PELHAM, LAVENDER ROAD, WILDWOOD CREST, N. J.

91817

An Avenue in Wildwood Crest, N. J.

An Avenue in Wildwood Crest.
A view of the large homes in Wildwood
Crest.

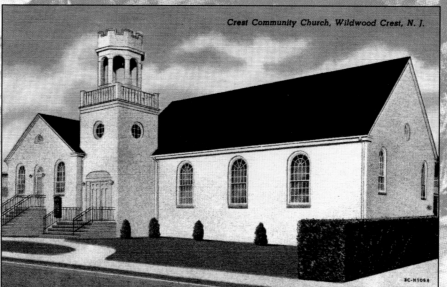

Crest Community Church, Wildwood Crest, N. J.

**Crest Community Church
is on Pacific Avenue.**

113

Sailing on Sunset Lake, Wildwood Crest. N. J.

Sailing is a favorite activity on Sunset Lake.

From the back: "Capt. George Sinn's BIG FLAMINGO, the Wildwoods' Largest Sightseeing Cruiser, 85 feet long!"

Fishing Party Returning Past the Rock Pile, Wildwood-by-the-Sea. This fishing party is coming through Cold Spring Inlet at the southern end of Wildwood Crest.

Fishing Party Returning Past the Rock Pile, Wildwood By the Sea, N. J.

105

This "Greetings from Cape May, New Jersey" postcard shows a little of everything!

Greetings from Cape May, New Jersey. This "Greetings" postcard shows four Cape May landmarks.

Light House

Congress Hall

Convention Hall

Greetings from CAPE MAY, N. J.

Beach & Boardwalk

AIRPLANE VIEW OF CAPE MAY. N. J.

An aerial view of Cape May.

Chapter Twelve:
Cape May

Cape May is the oldest of New Jersey's Southern Shore communities. Summer visitors were coming to Cape Island, as it was then called, before the American Revolution, and by the 1850s it was the most famous seaside resort in the country. The area was incorporated as the City of Cape May in 1869. In 1878, a fire destroyed thirty-five acres in the center of town, but it was quickly rebuilt and continued to be a fashionable summer resort.

After World War II, as the fortunes of the neighboring Wildwoods were on the upswing, Cape May was suffering a decline. Not until 1970, when the non-profit Mid-Atlantic Center for the Arts was founded to preserve the Emlen Physick Estate and other Victorian-era buildings from demolition, did Cape May once again become one of the great seaside resorts. In 1976, the City of Cape May was named a National Historic Landmark.

BOARDWALK AND BEACH FROM LAFAYETTE BATHS, CAPE MAY, N. J.

CONGRESS HALL, CAPE MAY, N.

Congress Hall, Cape May — it was the first large hotel built in Cape May.

The boardwalk and beach as seen from the Lafayette Baths, Cape May.

CONVENTION HALL, CAPE MAY, N. J.

BEACH AVENUE AND BOARDWALK, CAPE MAY, N. J.

Convention Hall, Cape May, New Jersey. Built by the city in 1917, it was open every evening during the season for free entertainment and dancing.

Beach Avenue and Boardwalk, Cape May. The Baby Parade strolls down the boardwalk as drivers, leaning against their vehicles, line up to see it.

The Cape May Hotel, built in the early 1900s, was one of the largest, and certainly the most expensive, hotels built in Cape May.

ADMIRAL HOTEL, CAPE MAY, N. J.

Admiral Hotel, Cape May. During the 1930s, the lifeguards held water circuses at the Admiral Hotel pool.

LAUNCHING THE LIFE BOAT, CAPE MAY, N. J.

Launching the Life Boat, Cape May, New Jersey. Cape May's beaches have always been well protected by lifeguards.

119

Post Office, Cape May, N. J.

Atlantic Studios, Cape May, N. J.   72073

The Post Office opened in December 1938 at the corner of Washington and Franklin Streets.

GREAT AIRSHIP HANGAR, NAVAL AIR STATION, CAPE MAY, N. J.

Great Airship Hangar, Naval Air Station, Cape May.
The Naval Air Station opened in November 1918. It housed a great dirigible.

PENNSYLVANIA R. R. STATION, CAPE MAY, N. J.

Baptist Church and Soldiers' Monument, Cape May, N. J.

Baptist Church and Soldiers' Monument, Cape May.
The Soldiers Monument in front of the Cape May Baptist Church at Columbia Avenue and Guerney Street was dedicated in 1923.

READING STATION, CAPE MAY, N. J.

Trains were extremely important in the development of Cape May, as these views demonstrate.

SCHELLENGER'S LANDING, CAPE MAY, N. J.

Schellenger's Landing, Cape May. **Schellenger's Landing is one of the most important fishing ports in Cape May County.**

Light House — Cape May Point, N.J.

Lighthouse by Moonlight, Cape May Point. The Cape May Lighthouse in Cape May Point was built in 1859. It is 157 ½ feet tall and has a distinctive beam that flashes every fifteen seconds. The beam is visible twenty-four miles out at sea.

This lighthouse is one of the most important lighthouses in New Jersey because it guides ships from the ocean through the treacherous entrance to the Delaware Bay.

Cape May Point from Lighthouse, Cape May, N. J.

219335

A view of Cape May Point from the lighthouse. The lighthouse stands on the most southerly point in New Jersey.

Chapter Thirteen: Cape May Point

Cape May Point, at the southernmost tip of New Jersey, is the site of a lighthouse built in 1859. Originally called Stites Beach after the Stites family, who owned the land, the area was established as the Sea Grove Association, a Presbyterian Retreat, in 1875 by John Wanamaker and Alexander Whildin. Whilden's wife was a member of the Stites family. The association banned all liquor and amusements. In 1878 Sea Grove was incorporated as the borough of Cape May Point. Wanamaker and his family summered in Cape May Point when he was the postmaster general in President Benjamin Harrison's cabinet, and he encouraged the President to visit the area, hoping to make Cape May Point the "summer White House."

Cape May Point, the smallest of the Southern Shore towns, is bordered on the east by Cape May Point State Park, on the south by the Atlantic Ocean, and on the west by the Delaware Bay. Fewer than three hundred people call Cape May Point home.

LILY LAKE, SHOWING LIGHT HOUSE IN BACKGROUND, CAPE MAY POINT, N. J.

Lily Lake, Showing Lighthouse in Background, Cape May Point. When Alexander Whildin and John Wanamaker founded the Sea Grove Association, they made Lily Lake the centerpiece of their Presbyterian Retreat. The lighthouse can be seen in the background of this view of Lake Lily.

FORMER RUSTIC BRIDGE AT LAKE LILY CAPE MAY POINT, N. J.

Former Rustic Bridge at Lake Lily, Cape May Point. During the War of 1812 British warships, guarding the mouth of the Delaware to prevent American ships from going up to Philadelphia, replenished their supply of fresh water from Lake Lily. Legend has it, seeing this, residents dug a trench connecting the lake with the ocean, making the lake salty. The trenches were later filled in and Lake Lily again became fresh.

CONCRETE SHIP ATLANTUS. CAPE MAY POINT, N. J.

Concrete Ship Atlantus, Cape May Point.
The concrete ship, *Atlantus*, was one of twelve experimental ships built during World War I when steel was scarce. It proved too heavy and too slow to be practical, however, and was sold to a company hoping to use it as a ferry landing. In 1926, during a storm, it broke from its mooring and was beached.

U. S. COAST GUARD LIFE SAVING STATION AND LIGHT HOUSE. CAPE MAY POINT, N. J.

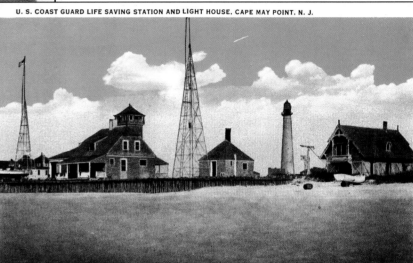

Delaware Bay Life Saving Station, Cape May, N. J.

LIFE SAVING STATION

A view of the U.S. Coast Guard Station, formerly the U.S. Life-Saving Station, on the left, the Cape May Lighthouse, and on the right the old Life-Saving Station. The older building was built for the 1876 Philadelphia Centennial Exposition. After the exposition the building was moved to Cape May Point.

Delaware Bay Life-Saving Station, Cape May.
The Life-Saving Station in Cape May Point was built in 1896 to replace an older, smaller station.

BEAUTIFUL SUNSET **ON** THE OCEAN, CAPE MAY POINT, N. J.

Searching for "Cape May Diamonds"

Beautiful Sunset on the Ocean, Cape May Point. Every evening during the season as the sun sets at Sunset Beach, a flag lowering ceremony is held. Each of the flags that fly over Sunset Beach is a veteran's casket flag, donated by the families.

CAPE MAY—LEWES
New Jersey   Delaware

Searching for "Cape May Diamonds" on Sunset Beach is a favorite pastime. Cape May Diamonds are small quartz pebbles, tumbled smooth by the ocean, that are transparent when wet.

The ferry between Cape May Point and Lewes, Delaware, began running in 1964. The ferry takes approximately seventy minutes to make its sixteen-mile journey across the Delaware Bay.

Bibliography

Beitel, Herbert M. and Enck, Vance C. *Cape May County: A Pictorial History*. Norfolk, Virginia: The Downing Company, 1988.

Boyer, George F. and Cunningham, J. Pearson. *Cape May County Story*. Egg Harbor City, New Jersey: The Laureate Press, 1975.

Burgess, Paul C. *Annals of Brigantine*. Atlantic City, New Jersey: Joseph Josephson and Son, 1964.

Cohen, Michael L. *Longport: The Way We Were*. Longport, New Jersey: Longport Historical Society, 1997.

Coskey, Dave. *Faces & Places from Avalon's Past*. Avalon, New Jersey: Avalonspast Publishing, 2002.

Field, Van R. and Galluzzo, John J. *New Jersey Coast Guard Stations and Rumrunners*. Charleston, South Carolina: Arcadia Publishing, 2004.

Francis, David W., Francis, Diane DeMali and Scully, Robert J. Sr. *Wildwood By-The-Sea*. Fairview Park, Ohio: Amusement Park Books, Inc., 1998.

Longport Historical Society. *Celebrating a Century of Incorporation as a Borough, 1898-1998*. Longport, New Jersey: The Beachcomber News and Printing Company, 1997.

Lurie, Maxine N. and Mappen, Marc. *Encyclopedia of New Jersey*. New Brunswick, New Jersey: Rutgers University Press, 2004.

McCann, Thomas P. *Lifeguarding in Sea Isle City Since 1882*. Bridgeton, New Jersey: Adams Printing, 2001.

McMahon, William. *So Young...So Gay, Story of the Boardwalk 1870-1970*. Atlantic City, New Jersey: Atlantic City Press, 1970.

Miller, Fred. *Ocean City: America's Greatest Family Resort*. Charleston, South Carolina: Arcadia Publishing, 2003.

Schaad, Jacob, Jr. and Scully, Robert J. Jr., with Vinci, Anna M. *North Wildwood: 100 Years Proud!* North Cape May, New Jersey: Printing Express, 2006.

Shanks, Ralph, York, Wick and Shanks, Lisa Woo, editor. *The U.S. Life-Saving Service-Heroes, Rescues and Architecture of the Early Coast Guard*. Petaluma, California: Costano Books, 1996.

Stafford, Michael F. *Sea Isle City*. Charleston, South Carolina: Arcadia Publishing, 2001.

Index

Aberdeen Hotel, 37
Absecon Lighthouse, 20
Admiral Hotel, 119
Atlantic City and Shore Railroad, 21, 34
Atlantic City Auditorium, 17
Atlantic City Racetrack, 21
Atlantus, 125
Avalon Hotel, 81
Avalon Pier, 78
Avalon Yacht Club, 81

Bayview Motel and Apartments, 61
Betty Bacharach Home for Afflicted Children, 39
Big Flamingo, 115
Bird Sanctuary, 90
Bonita Causeway, 6
Breakers Hotel, 19, 111
Brigantine Lighthouse, 9

Cannovas, Antonia "Jumbo," 73
Cape Baptist Church, 121
Cape May Diamonds, 126
Cape May Hotel, 119
Cape May Lighthouse, 122, 123
Chalfonte-Haddon Hall Hotel, 19
Church of the Blessed Sacrament, 33
Church of the Epiphany, 40
Church of the Redeemer, 40
Colonnade Hotel, 69
Concrete Ship, 125
Congress Hall, 118, 119
Convention Hall, 17, 118
Cold Spring Inlet, 115
Crest Community Church, 113
Crest Pier, 110, 111

Cronecker's Hotel and Café, 68

Deauville Inn, 59
Depot Hotel, 69
Devonshire Hotel, 37
Doughty's Pier, 44

Garden Pier, 14, 15
Gillian's Fun Deck, 50
Great Egg Inlet, 41

Harbor Theater, 89
Heinz Pier, 14
Hereford Inlet Lighthouse, 92
Hippodrome Pier, 45
Holly Beach, 99, 101
Hotel Biscayne, 55
Hotel Brigantine, 7
Hotel Davis, 105
Hotel Delaware, 55
Hotel Drayton, 105
Hotel Flanders, 45, 47, 54
Hunt's Starlight Ballroom, 104
Hygeia Pool, 17

Kennedy, John F. Memorial Bridge, 36

Inlet Hotel, 75

Jernee, Jack G., 47

Lafayette Baths, 118
Lake Lily, 124
Longport Wharf, 34, 35
Longport Boat, 35
Ludlam's Beach Lighthouse, 72
Lucy the Elephant, 29, 31, 32

Manor Hotel, 97
Marlborough-Blenheim Hotel, 18
Marvin Gardens, 31
Million Dollar Pier, 15
Music Pavilion, 44

Music Pier, 46, 47

Naval Air Station, 120
Normandie Hotel, 54

Ocean Bay Apartments, 38
Ocean City Beach Patrol Headquarters, 46, 47
Ocean City Yacht Club, 50, 51
Ocean Pier, 64, 65, 110
Otten's Harbor, 107
Oxford Apartments, 23

Pelham Hotel, 113
Pennsylvania and Reading Excursion Train, 56
Playland Amusements, 103
Playland Amusement Park, 50
Princeton Harbor, 80
Princeton Hotel, 83
Puriton Hotel, 82

Regent Theatre, 103

Sacred Heart Catholic Church, 83
Schellenger's Landing, 121
Sea Chest Apartments, 8
Sea Horse Pier, 6
Sea Isle City Amusement Parlor, 65
Sea Isle City Hospital, 71
Sea Isle City Yacht Club, 72
Seaspray Motel, 55
Seward Apartments, 110
Shore Fast Line, 21
Sindia, 49
Sportland Pool, 97
Steel Pier, 12, 14, 15
Steeplechase Pier, 14
Stone Harbor Beach Patrol, 86
Sunset Beach, 126
Sunset Lake, 114
Surf Hotel, 68
Surfside Hotel, 94, 95

Tabernacle Auditorium, 52

Traymore Hotel, 18

Unger, Elmer E., 49
U.S. Life-Saving Station, 9, 20, 48, 49, 56, 73, 74, 80, 86, 93, 100, 125

Ventnor Municipal Pier, 26
Ventnor Pier, 25, 26
Ventnor Recreation Pier, 26
Ventnor Water Works, 27
Villa Maria by the Sea Convent, 89

Whelen Hotel, 59
Widener Industrial School, 39

Zaberers, 97